JUNGLE BABIES
of the Amazon
Rain Forest

Capybaras

by **Rachel Lynette**

Consultant:
Dr. Mark C. Andersen
Department of Fish, Wildlife and Conservation Ecology
New Mexico State University

BEARPORT
PUBLISHING

New York, New York

Credits

Cover and Title, © Animals Animals/SuperStock; 4–5, © Paul Williams/naturepl.com; 6, 9, © Red Line Editorial; 6–7, 14–15, © Vadim Petrakov/Shutterstock Images; 8–9, 10–11, 23, © age fotostock/SuperStock; 10, 22, © Ian Rentoul/Shutterstock Images; 12, 22, © GlobetrotterJ/Shutterstock Images; 12–13, © Luiz Claudio Marigo/naturepl.com; 16, 23, © Richard Peterson/Shutterstock Images; 16–17, © Hung Chung Chih/Shutterstock Images; 18, © NHPA/SuperStock; 18–19, © Martina Berg/iStockphoto; 20–21, 23, © TOMO/Shutterstock Images.

Publisher: Kenn Goin
Editor: Joy Bean
Creative Director: Spencer Brinker
Photo Researcher: Arnold Ringstad
Design: Emily Love

Library of Congress Cataloging-in-Publication Data in process at time of publication (2013)
Library of Congress Control Number: 2012039854
ISBN-13: 978-1-61772-753-5 (library binding)

For more information, write to Bearport Publishing Company, Inc., 45 West 21st Street, Suite 3B, New York, New York 10010. Printed in the United States of America.

10 9 8 7 6 5 4 3 2 1

Contents

Meet a capybara family

After a day of swimming, the capybara family is tired.

The little ones, called pups, are only a few weeks old.

capybara pups

Soon they will climb on their mother's back and ride to a grassy area.

There the capybara family will take a nap.

capybara mother

All about capybaras

A capybara is a kind of **rodent**.

Some rodents, such as mice and squirrels, are small.

Capybaras, however, are the biggest rodents in the world.

An adult capybara is about the size of a Labrador retriever.

Adult capybara size

Where do capybaras live?

Capybaras live in the warm jungles of South America.

They spend most days in grassy areas near water.

capybara herd

Males, females, and pups live together in groups called herds.

Where capybaras live

North America

Atlantic Ocean

Pacific Ocean

South America

N W E S

Mother and pups

A mother capybara finds a hidden spot on land to give birth.

She hides so that **predators**, such as pumas and jaguars, can't find her babies.

jaguar

A mother has between four and eight pups at a time.

When a capybara is born, it weighs about three pounds (1.4 kg)—as much as three footballs.

mother capybara

capybara pup

Growing up

Baby capybaras can walk and swim when they are a few days old.

At first they drink milk from their mother's body.

After about a week, they start to eat grass, too.

All of the female capybaras in the herd work together to care for the babies.

caiman

They protect the pups from enemies such as **caimans** and large snakes called anacondas.

mother capybara

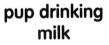
pup drinking milk

Important sounds

Young capybaras make loud purring noises.

Scientists think they do this to stay in touch with their herd.

Capybara pups, as well as adults, make clicking noises when they are happy.

capybara pups following their mother

When danger is nearby, they bark or cough to warn the herd.

Those who hear the noise run or jump into the water to stay safe.

capybara mother watching for danger

At home in the water

Capybaras are good swimmers.

Their **webbed** feet help them paddle through the water.

It is not unusual for capybara herds to spend whole days in rivers, lakes, and **swamps**.

There, the pups and adults eat water grasses and plants.

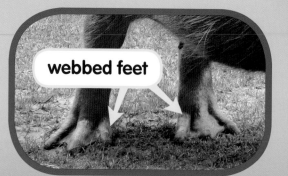

webbed feet

capybara
swimming

Hair and teeth

Capybara babies are like their parents.

They have long, thin hair that does not protect their skin from sunburn.

So they often roll around in mud to coat the skin.

Like the parents, their long, curved front teeth grow their entire lives.

Capybaras chew on tough grasses to keep the teeth worn down.

teeth

mud

All grown up

A capybara is fully grown when it is one year old.

By that time, it has learned to find its own food, swim, and stay safe.

The giant rodent is also ready to become a parent.

Like all capybaras, its pups will grow up and spend their lives with the herd.

adult
capybara

Glossary

caimans (KAY-muhnz) animals that are closely related to alligators

predators (PRED-uh-turs) animals that hunt and eat other animals

rodent (ROH-duhnt) a group of animals with large front teeth that includes rats, mice, squirrels, and capybaras

swamps (SWAHMPS) low areas of land that are mostly flooded and include areas of open water

webbed (WEBD) having toes connected by skin

Index

Read more

Ganeri, Anita. *Capybara (A Day in the Life: Rain Forest Animals).* Chicago: Heinemann-Raintree (2010).

Lunis, Natalie. *Capybara: The World's Largest Rodent (More Supersized!).* New York: Bearport Publishing (2010).

Manera, Alexandria. *Capybaras (Animals of the Rain Forest).* Chicago: Heinemann Library (2003).

Learn more online

To learn more about capybaras, visit
www.bearportpublishing.com/JungleBabies

About the author

Rachel Lynette has written more than 100 nonfiction books for children. She also creates resources for teachers. Rachel lives near Seattle, Washington. She enjoys biking, hiking, crocheting hats, and spending time with her family and friends.